Samsung Galaxy Z Flip 6
User Guide

A Comprehensive Manual with Large Print Instructions for Beginners and Seniors to Effectively Use and Customize the Foldable Smartphone

Felix Klein Wagner

Samsung Galaxy Z Flip 6 User Guide

Felix Klein Wagner

Disclaimer

This user guide is intended for informational and educational purposes only. While every effort has been made to ensure the accuracy, reliability, and completeness of the content, no guarantees are provided regarding its correctness or applicability to all users or situations.

The information presented in this guide is based on publicly available features and functionality of the Samsung Galaxy Z Flip 6. This manual is not affiliated with, endorsed by, or sponsored by Samsung Electronics Co., Ltd., its subsidiaries, or any related entities. All product names, trademarks, and brands mentioned are the property of their respective owners.

The author and publisher assume no responsibility or liability for any damages, malfunctions, or data loss resulting from the use or misuse of the information contained in this guide. Readers are encouraged to consult Samsung's official documentation, support services, or authorized providers for the most accurate and up-to-date information. Always follow Samsung's official instructions when setting up or operating your device.

Regarding Visuals

This manual is designed to offer clear, practical, and written instructions without the use of images, diagrams, or screenshots. This approach ensures the guide remains relevant, adaptable, and accessible, even as Samsung updates its software and interface.

For current visual references or device interface changes, users are encouraged to visit Samsung's official website or support pages. The absence of visuals allows this guide to be lightweight, easy to navigate, and inclusive for all types of readers.

With a focus on real-world usability, this guide is crafted to help you understand, personalize, and master your Samsung Galaxy Z Flip 6 with confidence and ease.

Why You Need This Guide

The **Samsung Galaxy Z Flip 6** is more than just a phone—it's a revolutionary device that blends cutting-edge technology with sleek, foldable design to offer an entirely new mobile experience. With its innovative features, powerful performance, and unique form factor, the Z Flip 6 sets itself apart from traditional smartphones. However, to fully unlock its potential and make the most of everything this device has to offer, you need more than just a quick glance at its functions.

This guide is your essential companion, crafted to help you navigate the device with ease, explore its many capabilities, and troubleshoot any challenges you might face. Whether you're a first-time foldable user or a seasoned Samsung enthusiast, this guide will ensure you:

- **Understand the Foldable Design**: Get to know the benefits of a foldable screen and how to maintain the durability of the Galaxy Z Flip 6.

- **Set Up Your Device**: Step-by-step instructions guide you through the setup process, from connecting to Wi-Fi to transferring data from your previous phone.

- **Master Essential Functions**: Learn how to make and receive calls, send texts, and manage your emails effectively—features that are essential in today's fast-paced world.

- **Explore Advanced Features**: Dive deep into the Z Flip 6's powerful camera, Flex Mode, and Samsung DeX capabilities. Unlock the true potential of the device with expert tips and tricks.

- **Troubleshoot with Confidence**: Quickly resolve common issues with easy-to-follow solutions and get support when needed, ensuring your device runs smoothly.

- **Stay Up to Date**: Keep your Z Flip 6 updated with the latest features and firmware, ensuring it remains cutting-edge and performs at its best.

This guide is designed not just to show you how to use your device, but to help you **maximize its capabilities** in every aspect of daily life. From taking stunning photos to multitasking with ease, the Samsung Galaxy Z Flip 6 is a powerful tool that you can use to enhance productivity, creativity, and entertainment. With this comprehensive guide in hand, you'll be equipped to get the most out of every fold, every feature, and every moment.

Your Z Flip 6 experience starts here—let's get the most out of it together.

Table of Contents

Introduction

Welcome to Your Samsung Galaxy Z Flip 6

Congratulations on your new Samsung Galaxy Z Flip 6! Whether you're upgrading to a foldable phone or exploring Samsung's latest innovation, you're about to experience the perfect blend of cutting-edge technology, performance, and style. The Z Flip 6 is designed to transform the way you interact with your device, offering an unparalleled mobile experience that adapts to your needs.

In this guide, you'll find everything you need to unlock the full potential of your Galaxy Z Flip 6. From setting it up to mastering its features, this guide ensures you have all the tools and tips you need to enjoy your phone to the fullest.

Key Features and Specifications

The Samsung Galaxy Z Flip 6 brings together sophisticated design, premium performance, and powerful functionality in a compact, foldable format. Below are some of the key features and specifications that set the Z Flip 6 apart:

- **Display**: The 6.7" Dynamic AMOLED 2X display provides vibrant colors, deep contrasts, and stunning clarity. Paired with the foldable design, it offers an experience that's both immersive and portable. The 120Hz refresh rate ensures smooth scrolling and seamless interaction.

- **Processor**: Powered by the latest Snapdragon 8 Gen 2 processor, the Z Flip 6 ensures fast, responsive performance whether you're multitasking, gaming, or streaming.

- **Battery Life**: The device includes a robust battery that supports up to a full day of use, with intelligent power-saving features that optimize battery consumption.

- **Camera**: With a 12 MP wide camera and a 12 MP ultra-wide lens, you can capture clear, detailed images and videos. Flex Mode enables unique hands-free photography and video recording.

- **Design**: The foldable design lets you enjoy a compact phone that unfolds into a full-screen experience. With Gorilla Glass Victus 2, the Z Flip 6 offers improved durability, and the hinge mechanism has been engineered for greater resilience.

- **5G Connectivity**: Enjoy ultra-fast download and upload speeds with the 5G connectivity, perfect for streaming, gaming, and more.

- **Storage**: Available in multiple storage configurations, you can choose the amount of space you need to store your apps, media, and documents.

Display: 6.7" Dynamic AMOLED & Foldable Design

The 6.7-inch Dynamic AMOLED 2X display is the centerpiece of the Galaxy Z Flip 6. This vibrant screen offers rich colors, deep contrasts, and sharp details for everything you view, from photos and videos to games and apps. The foldable design not only enhances portability but also provides an immersive experience when unfolded. Whether you're watching content or using apps, the stunning visuals are complemented by the smoothness of the 120Hz refresh rate.

The unique foldable feature allows you to enjoy a compact phone that easily fits into your pocket, while the expansive screen lets you open up to a tablet-like experience when you need it.

Performance: Processor & Battery Life

Under the hood, the Z Flip 6 is powered by the **Snapdragon 8 Gen 2** processor, ensuring that everything from daily tasks to high-performance apps runs seamlessly. The powerful chipset delivers smooth multitasking, fast app launches, and enhanced gaming experiences.

Battery life has also been optimized, so you can enjoy all the features of your Z Flip 6 throughout the day. With **optimized power management** and intelligent battery-saving features, the device adjusts its energy consumption based on your usage patterns, ensuring that you get the most out of every charge.

Camera Overview

The Samsung Galaxy Z Flip 6 is equipped with a **12 MP wide camera** and a **12 MP ultra-wide lens**, giving you the tools to capture stunning images in various settings. Whether you're shooting landscapes or close-up portraits, the Z Flip 6's cameras deliver vibrant, sharp photos and videos.

With **Flex Mode**, the Z Flip 6 offers a new way to shoot hands-free photos and videos, taking full advantage of the foldable form factor. Place your phone on a surface and use the device at different angles, making it perfect for selfies, group shots, or creative video angles.

The **Night Mode** ensures that your shots remain clear and detailed even in low-light conditions, while **Pro Mode** gives you manual control over camera settings, perfect for those who want more creative freedom. Whether you're a casual shooter or a photography enthusiast, the Z Flip 6's camera provides the flexibility to create professional-quality images.

What's in the Box?

When you unbox your Samsung Galaxy Z Flip 6, you'll find everything you need to get started with your new device. Here's what's included:

- **Samsung Galaxy Z Flip 6** – Your foldable smartphone, ready to go.
- **USB-C Charging Cable** – For fast charging and data transfer.
- **Wall Charger** (may vary by region) – For powering up your device quickly and safely.
- **SIM Ejector Tool** – For easy SIM card insertion and removal.
- **Quick Start Guide** – A brief guide to help you set up your device and get familiar with the basics.
- **Warranty Card** – Important information on your device's warranty and coverage.

Please note that some accessories, such as a wall charger or headphones, may not be included in all regions to reduce environmental impact. We recommend purchasing accessories from Samsung or authorized retailers to ensure compatibility and optimal performance.

Included Accessories & Optional Add-ons

Along with the essential components above, Samsung offers several **optional accessories** that you can purchase separately to enhance your Z Flip 6 experience. These include:

- **Samsung Wireless Charger** – Charge your Z Flip 6 wirelessly and effortlessly, with support for fast charging.

- **Samsung Protective Case** – Keep your device safe with a slim, durable case designed specifically for the Z Flip 6.

- **Samsung Clear Cover Case** – A sleek, transparent case that shows off your phone's foldable design while offering protection.

- **Screen Protector** – Ensure the longevity of your foldable screen by using a high-quality, Samsung-approved screen protector.

- **Galaxy Buds** – For immersive sound quality, pair your Z Flip 6 with Samsung's wireless earbuds.

- **Bluetooth Speakers or Headphones** – Take your music and entertainment to the next level with wireless audio accessories.

- **Car Charger** – Stay powered up on the go with a convenient car charger.

- **Samsung DeX Cable** – If you want to turn your Z Flip 6 into a desktop experience, you can purchase the Samsung DeX cable to connect your phone to a monitor, keyboard, and mouse.

Understanding the Foldable Design

The **Samsung Galaxy Z Flip 6**'s foldable design is not just a visual breakthrough—it's a practical innovation that brings new ways to interact with your smartphone. Unlike traditional smartphones, the Z Flip 6's flexible hinge allows it to fold in half, giving you a compact and portable phone that unfolds into a full 6.7-inch display when you need it.

This design is perfect for those who want the convenience of a pocket-sized device but still desire a larger screen for media consumption, browsing, or productivity. The foldable screen allows you to multitask with ease, offering features like **Flex Mode**, where the screen splits into two halves, letting you use apps simultaneously on the top and bottom sections. Whether you're watching a video while chatting or using a productivity app in split view, the foldable design offers endless possibilities.

The Flexibility & Durability of the Foldable Screen

Samsung's foldable screen is built to be both **flexible** and **durable**, ensuring it can handle daily use while maintaining its high-quality performance. The **Dynamic AMOLED 2X** display offers vibrant colors and excellent resolution, providing an immersive viewing experience whether the device is unfolded or folded. Despite its foldability, the screen is incredibly **resilient**, with **Gorilla Glass Victus 2** offering superior protection against scratches, drops, and other impacts.

Samsung has carefully engineered the hinge mechanism to ensure smooth folding and unfolding, with minimal wear over time. The Z Flip 6 has undergone extensive testing to ensure its durability, with the hinge designed for **over 200,000 folds** without significant degradation.

To keep your foldable screen in top shape, it's important to avoid placing excessive pressure on the screen when folding and unfolding the device. While the screen is designed to be durable, it's still a delicate component, so consider using **Samsung-approved screen protectors** to safeguard against scratches or other damage. Regularly cleaning the screen with a soft cloth will also help maintain its clarity.

Chapter 1

Getting Started

Turning Your Smartphone On and Off

Getting started with your **Samsung Galaxy Z Flip 6** is easy. Let's walk through the essential steps to turn your device on and off, and how to restart it if needed.

Turning the Device On & Off

1. **Powering On**:

   To turn on your Galaxy Z Flip 6, press and hold the **Power button** located on the right side of the device until the Samsung logo appears on the screen. Once the device powers up, you'll be greeted with the setup screen.

2. **Powering Off**:

   To power off your device, press and hold the **Power button** again. A menu will appear on the screen with options such as **Power off, Restart**, and **Emergency mode**. Select **Power off** and then tap **OK** to turn off your device. Wait for a few seconds, and the screen will turn off.

Restarting Your Device

If you encounter issues or want to refresh your device, you may need to restart it. Here's how to do that:

1. Press and hold the **Power button** until the menu appears.

2. Select **Restart** from the menu.

3. Tap **Restart** again to confirm, and your device will reboot.

Restarting can help resolve minor issues like frozen apps or sluggish performance. It's a good practice to restart your device periodically for optimal performance.

Setting Up Your Phone

Follow these steps to configure your phone for the first time:

1. **Language & Region Setup**:

   Choose your preferred language and region. This will determine the language used on your device and adjust settings such as the time zone and currency.

2. **Wi-Fi & Mobile Network Setup**:

   After selecting your language and region, the phone will prompt you to connect to a Wi-Fi network. Select your Wi-Fi network from the list, enter the password, and your phone will automatically connect. If you want to use mobile data, you can skip this step or select your mobile network provider when prompted.

3. **Samsung Account Setup**:

   Signing into your Samsung account allows you to access various Samsung services, such as Samsung Cloud, Samsung Health, and the Galaxy Store. If you don't have a Samsung account yet, you can create one by following the on-screen instructions. Signing in ensures that your data is backed up and synced across your Samsung devices.

4. **Google Account Setup**:

After your Samsung account setup, you'll be prompted to sign into your Google account. This is required for accessing Google Play Store, Gmail, Google Photos, and other Google services. If you don't already have a Google account, you can create one during the setup process.

Wi-Fi, Mobile Network, & Samsung Account Setup

When you first set up your Z Flip 6, it's essential to connect to a Wi-Fi network for an optimal setup experience. Wi-Fi helps you download apps, update software, and back up your data efficiently.

1. **Wi-Fi Setup**:

   ○ On the setup screen, you'll see available Wi-Fi networks. Select your network and enter your Wi-Fi password to connect.

   ○ If you have any issues with Wi-Fi connectivity, you can try moving closer to the router or restarting your device.

2. **Mobile Network Setup**:

   ○ If you don't have access to Wi-Fi, you can connect using your mobile network. Ensure that your SIM card is properly inserted, and your network provider's settings will automatically configure your connection.

   ○ For **dual SIM** users, the Z Flip 6 will prompt you to select a default SIM for data, voice calls, and messaging.

3. **Samsung Account Setup**:

   Signing in with your Samsung account not only gives you access to Samsung-exclusive features, but it also helps you sync your settings, apps, and content across Samsung devices. If you're new to Samsung, creating an account is quick and easy through the setup wizard.

Transferring Data from Your Old Device

If you're upgrading from another phone, the **Samsung Smart Switch** app makes transferring your data a seamless process. Here's how to move your contacts, messages, photos, and apps to your new Z Flip 6:

1. **Install Samsung Smart Switch** on your old device if it's not already installed (it's available on both Android and iOS).

2. **Connecting the Devices**:

   ○ For Android to Android transfer, simply connect the two devices using a USB cable or use Wi-Fi. If you're transferring from an iPhone, follow the on-screen instructions to pair both devices.

○ You may need to enter a **security PIN** or **password** to authorize the transfer.

3. **Select Data to Transfer**:

   Once connected, choose the type of data you'd like to transfer. You can select contacts, messages, photos, videos, apps, and even settings.

4. **Begin Transfer**:

   After selecting your data, press **Transfer**. The process might take a few minutes depending on the amount of data being moved.

5. **Complete Setup**:

   After the transfer is complete, your Z Flip 6 will have your old data ready to go. If any apps need to be re-downloaded, you'll be prompted to do so from the **Google Play Store**.

Inserting SIM & MicroSD Cards

To get started with your Samsung Galaxy Z Flip 6, you need to insert the **SIM card** and optionally, a **MicroSD card** (if supported for additional storage). Here's how to do it:

1. **Locate the SIM Tray**:

   The SIM tray is located on the right side of your device, just below the power button.

2. **Eject the SIM Tray**:

Insert the **SIM ejector tool** (included in the box) into the small hole next to the tray. Apply gentle pressure to pop out the tray.

3. **Insert the SIM Card**:

Place your **nano SIM card** into the tray, ensuring that it fits snugly and aligns with the metal contacts. If your device supports a **MicroSD card**, insert it in the other slot (if available), following the same steps.

4. **Reinsert the Tray**:

Slide the tray back into the device, making sure it's fully inserted. Your Galaxy Z Flip 6 should automatically detect the SIM card and mobile network.

Charging Your Device

Your Samsung Galaxy Z Flip 6 requires charging to stay powered throughout the day. You can charge your device in several ways, including via USB-C, wireless charging, and reverse wireless charging.

1. **USB-C Charging**:
   - **Connect the Charging Cable**: Plug the **USB-C charging cable** into the USB-C port on your device. Connect the other end to a compatible **wall charger**.

   - **Charging Indicator**: When charging, you'll see a battery icon in the status bar, indicating the charging progress. You can also see the percentage of charge on the lock screen.

2. **Wireless Charging**:
   - **Place Your Device on a Wireless Charger**: To charge wirelessly, place your device on a **Qi-compatible wireless charging pad**. Ensure that your device is centered on the pad for optimal charging efficiency.

   - **Charging Speed**: The Z Flip 6 supports fast wireless charging, so you can expect your device to charge relatively quickly without needing to plug it in.

3. **Reverse Wireless Charging**:
   - **PowerShare Feature**: If you need to charge other devices (like a pair of **Galaxy Buds** or another phone), you can use the **Wireless PowerShare** feature. Simply enable it from the quick settings menu and place the other device on the back of your Z Flip 6.

   - **Charging Setup**: To start, swipe down from the top of the screen to access the quick settings menu, tap on **Wireless PowerShare**, and place the devices back-to-back.

Basic Navigation

Your Samsung Galaxy Z Flip 6 uses **One UI** to make navigation smooth and intuitive. Here's a quick guide to navigating the system:

1. **Home Button and Navigation Bar**:

- Home Button: Tap the **Home button** to go to your main screen from anywhere.

- **Back Button**: Tap the **Back button** to go to the previous screen or exit apps.

- **Recent Apps Button**: Tap the **Recent apps button** to see all open apps and switch between them.

2. **Gestures for Navigation** (Optional):

You can also use **gesture controls** to navigate. Swipe up from the bottom to go to the home screen, swipe up and hold for recent apps, or swipe from the left or right edge to go back.

Home Screen & App Drawer Customization

Your Galaxy Z Flip 6's **Home Screen** and **App Drawer** can be personalized to make the experience truly yours. Here's how you can customize them:

1. **Customizing the Home Screen**:
   - **Adding Apps to the Home Screen**: To add apps to the home screen, open the **App Drawer** (by swiping up from the bottom of the screen), then press and hold the app you want to add and drag it to your desired location on the home screen.

   - **Creating Folders**: To organize your apps, you can create **folders**. Simply drag one app over another to create a folder, and you can name the folder for easy identification.

- ○ **Changing Wallpaper**: Press and hold an empty area on the home screen, then tap **Wallpapers** to change your wallpaper to a new image or design. You can use static or dynamic wallpapers that update throughout the day.

- ○ **Widgets**: Tap and hold an empty space on the home screen, then select **Widgets**. Choose from various widgets like clock, calendar, or news updates to place on your home screen.

2. **Customizing the App Drawer**:
   - ○ **Organizing Apps**: You can organize the apps in your App Drawer alphabetically or by frequently used. To customize, open the **App Drawer**, tap the three vertical dots in the upper-right corner, and select **Sort**. You can also hide apps you don't want to see by tapping **Hide Apps** in the App Drawer settings.

   - ○ **Searching Apps**: If you have many apps, swipe down in the App Drawer to reveal a search bar where you can type the name of the app you're looking for.

3. **Changing the App Icons**:
   You can also change the appearance of your apps:

○ Go to **Settings** > **Display** > **Icon Shape** to choose between a variety of icon styles, such as round or square.

○ **Icon Packs**: If you want a completely different look, you can download and apply **icon packs** through the Galaxy Store.

Chapter 2

Display Features

Flex Mode: Unlocking Hands-Free Viewing

One of the standout features of your **Samsung Galaxy Z Flip 6** is **Flex Mode**, which allows you to use your device hands-free by taking full advantage of its foldable design. Flex Mode transforms the way you interact with your device, enabling you to use apps in a more flexible and intuitive way. Here's how it works and why it's so useful:

1. **How to Activate Flex Mode**:

   Simply fold your Galaxy Z Flip 6 at a 90-degree angle, and Flex Mode will automatically activate in compatible apps. The screen is split into two sections—use the top portion for viewing content while the bottom half remains interactive for controls or typing.

2. **Hands-Free Usage**:

   Flex Mode is perfect for video calls, group selfies, and watching videos while multitasking. You can comfortably position your phone on a flat surface, allowing you to use it without holding it, making it ideal for video chats or hands-free video viewing.

3. **Enhanced Multitasking**:

   Flex Mode makes multitasking more efficient. While watching a video, you can use the lower half of the screen to send messages, scroll through social media, or take notes, all while keeping your screen and workflow separated.

Benefits & App Compatibility

Flex Mode isn't just a fun feature—it's designed to make your daily interactions with your Galaxy Z Flip 6 more productive and enjoyable. Here are some benefits and details on app compatibility:

1. **Video Calls**:

   With Flex Mode, you can hold a video call and have both participants clearly visible in the top half of the screen while typing in the bottom half, all without holding your phone. Apps like **Google Duo** and **Samsung Video Call** take full advantage of this mode.

2. **YouTube & Video Streaming**:

   Flex Mode enhances your YouTube experience by allowing you to watch videos while interacting with the app's controls. The video plays in the top half of the screen, and you can use the bottom half for comments, likes, or browsing other videos.

3. **Productivity Apps**:

   Apps like **Google Docs** and **Samsung Notes** allow for more efficient multitasking. You can edit documents or jot down notes in the bottom half while reading or referencing something in the top half, increasing your productivity without switching between apps.

4. **Photography & Selfies**:

   Flex Mode makes it easier to take selfies, especially group shots. Simply fold the phone to the desired angle, and the bottom screen functions as a live preview, while the top portion shows the camera viewfinder.

5. **App Compatibility**:

   Many Samsung apps are optimized for Flex Mode, including **Samsung Video**, **Google Photos**, **Google Meet**, and **WhatsApp**. Over time, additional apps will continue to incorporate this feature, enhancing your experience.

The Main Display

The **6.7-inch Dynamic AMOLED 2X** main display is the heart of your Samsung Galaxy Z Flip 6. It offers vibrant colors, sharp resolution, and a smooth 120Hz refresh rate. Here are the key features and customization options for this powerful screen:

1. **High-Resolution Display**:

   With a resolution of **2640 x 1080 pixels**, the main display offers crystal-clear clarity for everything from videos and games to apps and documents. Enjoy immersive visuals whether you're watching a movie or browsing the web.

2. **120Hz Refresh Rate**:

   The **120Hz refresh rate** ensures that everything from scrolling through social media to gaming remains fluid and smooth. Whether you're flipping through your apps or watching a high-speed sports game, the refresh rate adapts to the content for the best experience.

3. **Color Accuracy**:

Samsung's **Dynamic AMOLED 2X** display provides rich, accurate colors, with vibrant contrasts and deep blacks, making your content come to life. The display is HDR10+ certified, offering enhanced brightness and color for video content.

4. **Eye Comfort**:

Blue Light Reduction mode is available, which adjusts the color temperature to reduce blue light and protect your eyes during prolonged screen time. You can customize this in **Settings > Display > Blue Light Filter**.

Display Settings: Brightness, Color, & Screen Timeout

To get the most out of your Galaxy Z Flip 6's display, you can fine-tune settings such as brightness, color modes, and screen timeout. Here's how:

1. **Adjusting Brightness**:
   - **Manual Brightness**: Go to **Settings > Display > Brightness** to adjust the brightness manually for your comfort. You can also swipe down the notification panel and use the slider to adjust brightness quickly.

   - **Adaptive Brightness**: This feature automatically adjusts the screen brightness based on your surrounding light conditions. Enable it by going to **Settings > Display > Adaptive Brightness**, which helps save battery life in varying environments.

2. **Color Mode**:

The Galaxy Z Flip 6 offers a variety of color modes to suit your personal preference:

  ○ **Vivid Mode**: Enhances color saturation for a richer viewing experience.

  ○ **Natural Mode**: Provides more balanced colors, ideal for users who prefer less intense color saturation.

3. To change the color mode, navigate to **Settings** > **Display** > **Screen Mode** and choose between **Vivid** or **Natural**.

4. **Screen Timeout**:

Screen timeout determines how long the display stays on after you stop interacting with it. To save battery or reduce distractions, you can adjust the screen timeout settings:

  ○ Go to **Settings** > **Display** > **Screen Timeout** and select a time between 15 seconds and 30 minutes.

Cover Display

The **Cover Display** on your Samsung Galaxy Z Flip 6 offers a sleek and convenient way to access essential information without having to unfold your device. This compact screen gives you a quick overview of notifications, time, and other vital info at a glance, making it easier to stay connected while keeping your device compact and portable.

1. **Quick Notifications**:

   With the Cover Display, you can easily check incoming notifications such as messages, emails, calls, and app alerts. Instead of opening your phone, simply glance at the cover screen to see a preview of any notifications. Tap the notification to open the associated app or swipe to dismiss it.

2. **Music Controls**:

   If you're listening to music or a podcast, the Cover Display allows you to control playback without unfolding the device. You can pause, play, skip tracks, or adjust volume directly from the cover screen.

3. **Camera Preview**:

   The Cover Display also serves as a useful tool for taking selfies. Simply open the camera app, and the cover screen shows you a preview of your photo, allowing you to adjust your framing before capturing the shot.

4. **Quick Settings**:

   Access frequently used settings directly from the Cover Display, including Wi-Fi, Bluetooth, and Do Not Disturb modes. It's a great way to toggle key functions without unfolding your phone.

Viewing Notifications & Quick Settings

The **Cover Display** not only shows notifications but also provides a quick way to access essential settings. Here's how to make the most out of it:

1. **Viewing Notifications**:

   When you receive notifications, the **Cover Display** shows a preview of the message or alert. You can tap on the notification to open the associated app or swipe right to dismiss it. For emails, texts, and social media updates, you can see the subject line and a brief preview of the content.

2. **Replying to Messages**:

   For a more interactive experience, you can reply to messages directly from the Cover Display. When you receive a text or message notification, swipe up to open a quick reply interface, and type your response. This feature allows you to respond without unfolding your phone, making it more convenient when you're on the go.

3. **Quick Settings Menu**:

   You can access essential settings right from the Cover Display. Swiping down from the top of the screen brings up the quick settings menu, where you can toggle features like:

   - **Wi-Fi**
   - **Bluetooth**
   - **Sound Mode**
   - **Do Not Disturb**

o **Battery Saver**

4. This feature makes it easier to make adjustments without fully opening your phone, perfect for when you need to change settings quickly while on the move.

Always On Display

The **Always On Display (AOD)** is a powerful feature that ensures key information is always visible, even when your Galaxy Z Flip 6 is locked. This feature can be particularly helpful for checking the time, notifications, or battery level without having to unlock your device.

1. **What's Displayed**:
   With AOD enabled, your screen will continuously show essential details, such as:

   o **Time & Date**
   o **Battery Level**
   o **Notifications** (text messages, emails, app updates)
   o **Music/Media Controls**
   o **Calendar Events**

2. AOD is customizable, so you can choose exactly what information you want to see, whether it's a simple clock or a more detailed layout with notifications and media controls.

3. **Customizing Always On Display**:

To customize what's displayed on your AOD screen, follow these steps:

  ○ Go to **Settings > Lock Screen > Always On Display**.

  ○ Choose between different clock styles (digital, analog, or other designs).

  ○ Decide whether you want additional information like notifications or calendar events to appear on the screen.

4. **Battery Saving with AOD**:

While the Always On Display is a handy feature, it can drain your battery if left on continuously. However, you can adjust settings to optimize its performance:

  ○ **Tap to Show**: You can set AOD to only display when you tap the screen, reducing power usage.

  ○ **Schedule AOD**: Set specific hours for AOD to be active, such as during the day or night, to save battery life.

5. **Turning Off Always On Display**:

If you prefer not to use AOD, you can easily disable it by going to **Settings > Lock Screen > Always On Display**, and turning off the toggle. You can also turn it off temporarily by setting it to display only when you tap the screen.

Chapter 3

Making Calls, Sending Texts & Emails

Making and Receiving Calls

Your **Samsung Galaxy Z Flip 6** is equipped with all the features you need for making and receiving calls, ensuring you stay connected with ease. Here's how to manage your calls:

1. **Making a Call**:

   To make a call, open the **Phone** app by tapping on the phone icon on your home screen or app drawer. You can make calls in three ways:

   - **Dial Pad**: Use the dial pad to manually enter a phone number.
   - **Contacts**: Tap on the **Contacts** tab and select the contact you wish to call.
   - **Recent Calls**: Go to the **Recents** tab to find a recently dialed number and tap it to redial.

2. **Answering a Call**:

   When you receive a call, the **incoming call screen** will appear. You can answer the call by swiping the green **Answer** button. If you prefer not to answer, you can swipe the red **Decline** button to reject the call.

3. **Ending a Call**:

   To end the call, tap the **End Call** button on the screen. You can also press the **Power button** to hang up if you're using hands-free options like a Bluetooth headset or speaker.

Using the Dialer & Video Calls

The **Phone** app also allows you to make **video calls**, providing a face-to-face connection even when you're far apart. Here's how to use both the dialer and video calls:

1. **Using the Dialer**:
   - Open the **Phone** app and tap the **Dialer** tab at the bottom.

   - Enter the number you wish to call, or search for a contact from your **Contacts** list.

   - Once you've entered the number, tap the green **Call** button to initiate the call.

2. **Making a Video Call**:
   The Z Flip 6 supports video calling via several apps, including **Google Duo**, **Samsung Video Call**, and third-party apps like **Zoom** and **WhatsApp**.

   - To make a video call, go to your **Contacts** or **Dialer** and select the contact you want to call.

○ Tap on the **video call icon** (usually a camera symbol) next to the contact name.

○ If the contact also supports video calling, the video call will begin once they answer. You can toggle between the front and rear cameras during the call if needed.

Texting: Messages & Multimedia

Texting on your Galaxy Z Flip 6 is easy and efficient with the **Messages** app. Whether you're sending plain SMS messages, multimedia (MMS), or group texts, this guide covers all you need to know:

1. **Sending an SMS**:
    ○ Open the **Messages** app, and tap on the **New Message** icon (usually a pencil or plus symbol).

    ○ Enter the recipient's phone number or tap the contact name to choose from your contacts.

    ○ Type your message in the text field at the bottom and tap **Send** to send your SMS.

2. **Sending MMS (Multimedia Messages)**:

- MMS messages let you send photos, videos, audio, and other media. To send an MMS:

  - Open a conversation in **Messages**, or start a new one.

  - Tap the **attachment icon** (paperclip) and select the type of media you want to send (photo, video, audio, etc.).

  - Choose the media from your phone and tap **Send**.

- Note: MMS messaging requires a mobile data connection. Ensure **Mobile Data** is turned on in your settings.

3. **Sending Group Texts**:

Group texting lets you communicate with multiple people at once. Here's how to set up and send group texts:

- Open the **Messages** app and tap **New Message**.

- Enter multiple contacts in the recipient field, or select them from your contacts list.

- Type your message as you normally would and tap **Send**.

- Group texts allow everyone in the group to see and respond to each other's messages. Keep in mind that depending on your carrier, group texting may be sent as individual messages or as a single thread with all participants' replies.

4. **Managing Group Conversations**:
   You can customize group texts by tapping on the group name at the top of the conversation to rename the group, mute notifications, or remove contacts. For more advanced options, such as leaving a group, you can access the settings within the conversation.

Email Setup & Management

Setting up your email accounts on your **Samsung Galaxy Z Flip 6** is straightforward, and managing your inbox is made easy with the **Samsung Email** app or any third-party email service you prefer. Here's how to get started:

Adding Accounts

1. **Opening the Email App**:
   - Open the **Email** app by tapping on the envelope icon from your home screen or app drawer.

2. **Adding a New Account**:
   - If you're setting up your email for the first time, the app will prompt you to add an email account.

   - Tap **Add Account**, and choose your email provider (Google, Outlook, Yahoo, etc.), or select **Other** for custom configurations.

○ For **Google accounts**, simply sign in using your Gmail address and password. If you're adding a different email provider, enter your email address and password. You may be asked to enter additional server settings (IMAP/POP3 and SMTP) for certain email providers.

3. **Sync Settings**:

○ Once your account is added, you can adjust the sync settings for your account. You can choose how often your device checks for new emails, whether to sync contacts and calendar events, and if you want to sync attachments.

○ Tap **Settings** (the gear icon), then select your email account, and choose the sync options according to your preferences.

4. **Multiple Accounts**:

○ If you have more than one email account, you can easily switch between them. In the **Email** app, tap the **menu icon** (three horizontal lines) in the upper-left corner and select the account you want to view. To add more accounts, tap **Add Account** and follow the same process.

Organizing Inboxes

1. **Folders & Labels**:

To keep your inbox organized, use folders or labels to categorize emails.

○ **Create Folders**: In the **Email** app, tap the **three dots menu** in the upper-right corner, select **Manage Folders**, and then tap **Create Folder**. You can create different folders for work, personal emails, or any custom organization you prefer.

○ **Move Emails to Folders**: To move an email, tap on the email you want to move, select the **three dots** in the upper-right corner, and choose **Move to Folder**. Select the folder where you'd like to store the email.

2. **Using the Search Function**:

○ If you need to find a specific email, use the **search bar** at the top of the inbox. Simply type in keywords, the sender's name, or an email subject to locate the email quickly.

3. **Marking Emails**:
○ You can **star** or **flag** important emails for easy reference. Tap the **star icon** next to the email to mark it as important.

○ You can also **archive** emails to keep them organized without deleting them. Archived emails can be found in the **All Mail** folder.

Sending Attachments

1. **Composing an Email**:

○ To compose a new email, tap the **plus icon** or **Compose** button in the lower-right corner of the **Email** app. Enter the recipient's email address, subject, and message.

2. **Adding Attachments**:

To add attachments like photos, documents, or files to your email:

○ In the **Compose** screen, tap the **paperclip icon** or **Attach** button.
○ You can select attachments from various sources, such as:

- **Gallery** (for photos and videos)
- **Documents** (for PDFs, Word files, etc.)
- **Drive** (for cloud storage files)

○ After selecting your attachment, it will appear below the text field in your email.

3. **Sending Emails with Attachments**:

After you've written your message and attached any files, tap **Send** to send the email. Be mindful of the file size limit—most email providers have restrictions on attachment sizes (usually around 25MB).

4. **Adding Multiple Attachments**:

You can add multiple attachments by repeating the above steps, selecting additional files to attach. Just ensure the total file size is within the allowed limits of your email provider.

Chapter 4

Connectivity

Wi-Fi, Bluetooth & Mobile Data Setup

Setting up your **Wi-Fi**, **Bluetooth**, and **Mobile Data** on your Samsung Galaxy Z Flip 6 ensures seamless connectivity for browsing, communication, and more. Here's how to get connected:

1. **Wi-Fi Setup**:
   - **Connecting to Wi-Fi**:
     To connect to a Wi-Fi network, swipe down from the top of the screen to open the **Quick Settings** panel. Tap the **Wi-Fi** icon to enable Wi-Fi. Then, select your network from the list of available networks and enter the Wi-Fi password. Your device will automatically connect once the password is entered correctly.

   - **Managing Wi-Fi Networks**:
     Go to **Settings > Connections > Wi-Fi** to view available networks, manage saved networks, or forget a network you no longer use.

   - **Advanced Wi-Fi Settings**:
     For advanced settings like managing the frequency band (2.4GHz vs. 5GHz) or configuring a proxy, tap **Wi-Fi > More Options (three dots) > Advanced**. Here, you can fine-tune your Wi-Fi setup for optimal performance.

2. **Bluetooth Setup**:

   ○ **Turning Bluetooth On**:

   To enable Bluetooth, swipe down the notification panel and tap the **Bluetooth** icon. Alternatively, go to **Settings > Connections > Bluetooth**, and toggle the switch to turn it on.

   ○ **Pairing Bluetooth Devices**:

   Once Bluetooth is enabled, your Z Flip 6 will scan for available devices. Tap on the device you want to connect to, such as wireless headphones, speakers, or car systems. Confirm the pairing by accepting the prompt on both your phone and the paired device. Once connected, you can use the device for audio, file transfer, and more.

   ○ **Managing Bluetooth Connections**:

   To manage your connected devices, go to **Settings > Connections > Bluetooth**, where you can disconnect, remove, or reconnect previously paired devices.

3. **Mobile Data Setup**:

   ○ **Enabling Mobile Data**:

   To use mobile data, swipe down the notification panel and tap the **Mobile Data** icon to turn it on. Alternatively, go to **Settings > Connections > Data usage**, and toggle **Mobile data** on.

   ○ **Configuring Data Settings**:

   Under **Settings > Connections > Data usage**, you can track your data usage, set data limits, and adjust settings to avoid exceeding your mobile data allowance.

- ○ **Managing Roaming**:

  If you're traveling internationally, you may need to enable **Data Roaming** to continue using mobile data. Go to **Settings > Connections > Mobile networks > Data roaming**, and toggle it on.

Managing Connections & Mobile Hotspot

Managing your device's connections effectively ensures that you stay connected whether you're at home, work, or on the go. Here's how to manage your connections and use your phone as a mobile hotspot:

1. **Managing Wi-Fi Connections**:
   - ○ **Switching Between Networks**:

     Your device can automatically switch between available Wi-Fi networks, but you can manually select which network to connect to by going to **Settings > Connections > Wi-Fi**.

   - ○ **Wi-Fi Sharing**:

     Share your Wi-Fi network with others by enabling **Wi-Fi Direct**, a feature that allows fast, peer-to-peer connection. You can find it under **Settings > Connections > Wi-Fi > Wi-Fi Direct**.

2. **Mobile Hotspot**: The **Mobile Hotspot** feature allows you to share your phone's mobile data connection with other devices like laptops, tablets, and

other smartphones.

- ○ **Turning on Mobile Hotspot**:

  To set up your mobile hotspot, go to **Settings > Connections > Mobile Hotspot and Tethering**. Toggle the **Mobile Hotspot** option to enable it.

- ○ **Customizing Hotspot Settings**:

  You can customize your hotspot by changing the network name (SSID), password, and security settings. To do this, tap **Mobile Hotspot** and then **Configure**.

- ○ **Data Usage**:

  Keep track of your mobile hotspot data usage in the **Mobile Hotspot and Tethering** menu, and set data limits to ensure you don't exceed your plan's data allowance.

3. **Tethering**: Tethering allows you to share your mobile data connection with other devices through a USB cable or Bluetooth.

   - ○ **USB Tethering**:

     Connect your Z Flip 6 to a computer via USB, then go to **Settings > Connections > Mobile Hotspot and Tethering**, and enable **USB Tethering**.

   - ○ **Bluetooth Tethering**:

     Pair your phone with a Bluetooth-enabled device, then enable

Bluetooth Tethering in the same menu to share your data connection wirelessly.

NFC & Samsung Pay

The **Samsung Galaxy Z Flip 6** supports **NFC (Near Field Communication)** for easy payments and data transfer. Here's how to use NFC and set up **Samsung Pay** for fast, secure transactions:

1. **Using NFC**: NFC is a short-range communication technology that allows your device to transfer data or make payments with a simple tap.

   - **Enabling NFC**:
     To enable NFC, go to **Settings > Connections > NFC and payment**, and toggle the NFC option to **On**.

   - **Using NFC for File Transfer**:
     With NFC enabled, you can easily share photos, contacts, and other files between compatible devices by bringing the backs of the two phones together. Tap the NFC area (typically the back of your phone) to initiate the transfer.

2. **Samsung Pay: Quick & Secure Payments**: Samsung Pay allows you to make contactless payments using your Galaxy Z Flip 6. It's accepted by millions of retailers worldwide, making it a convenient and secure way to pay.

○ **Setting Up Samsung Pay**:

To set up Samsung Pay, open the **Samsung Pay** app from your app drawer. Follow the on-screen instructions to add your credit or debit card details. You may need to verify your identity using your fingerprint, PIN, or iris scan.

○ **Making a Payment**:

Once your card is added, swipe up from the home screen to open Samsung Pay. Hold your phone near the contactless payment terminal, and authenticate the transaction using **fingerprint** or **PIN** verification.

○ **Using Samsung Pay with NFC**:

With NFC enabled, Samsung Pay uses NFC technology to make quick, secure payments. Just ensure that your NFC is turned on and that the retailer supports **contactless payments**.

Connecting to Samsung DeX

Samsung **DeX** (Desktop Experience) transforms your Galaxy Z Flip 6 into a **desktop-like experience**, allowing you to connect your phone to a monitor, keyboard, and mouse for enhanced productivity and convenience. Here's how you can get started with Samsung DeX:

1. **Getting Started with DeX**:

○ **Wired Connection**:

To use DeX with a wired connection, you'll need a **USB-C to HDMI**

cable or a **Samsung DeX Station/Pad**. Connect your Galaxy Z Flip 6 to a monitor using the appropriate cable.

- ○ **Wireless Connection**:

  If you prefer a wireless connection, ensure that both your Galaxy Z Flip 6 and the compatible TV or monitor support **Miracast**. Make sure both devices are connected to the same Wi-Fi network. Then, swipe down the notification panel on your phone and select **Samsung DeX** from the quick settings. Tap **Start DeX** to wirelessly connect to the monitor or TV.

2. **Setting Up DeX on a Monitor or TV**:
   - ○ Once connected via HDMI or wirelessly, your phone's display will shift to the external monitor, and you'll see a desktop-like environment where you can use apps in resizable windows, drag and drop files, and more.

   - ○ If using a **DeX Station**, you may need to connect a **keyboard** and **mouse** via USB ports on the DeX device. With a wireless setup, you can connect Bluetooth-enabled peripherals (keyboard and mouse) directly to your Galaxy Z Flip 6.

3. **Navigating DeX Mode**:
   - ○ **Taskbar**: Just like on a desktop, you'll see a taskbar at the bottom of the screen where you can access your apps, open recent apps, and manage system settings.

○ **Multi-Window**: Open multiple apps in resizable windows. You can drag and drop windows, minimize or maximize them, and work more efficiently.

○ **App Compatibility**: Most Android apps are compatible with DeX, but some may not support full desktop functionality. However, most Google apps (like Gmail, Docs, Sheets, etc.) and Samsung's own suite of apps are fully optimized for DeX.

4. **Using DeX for Productivity**:

○ You can use the **Microsoft Office** suite, **Google Workspace**, and other productivity apps just as you would on a traditional desktop computer. Edit documents, create presentations, or manage spreadsheets on a large screen with a keyboard and mouse, offering you a truly mobile workspace.

File Management & Display Setup

Once you're connected to Samsung DeX, managing your files and adjusting your display settings is simple. Here's how to manage files and optimize your DeX setup:

1. **File Management on DeX**:

○ **Accessing Files**:
You can manage your files through the **Samsung My Files** app, which allows you to browse and organize your internal storage, SD card (if

applicable), and cloud storage. You can drag and drop files between different locations, such as your device storage and external storage drives (USB, SD card).

- ○ **Transferring Files**:
  - ■ **Between Phone and PC**: You can transfer files between your Galaxy Z Flip 6 and your PC by dragging them from the DeX desktop to your PC's file explorer window (if you have both devices connected to the same network or via USB).

  - ■ **External Storage**: To access external storage like a USB flash drive, plug the drive into the USB port of your **DeX Station** (if using a wired setup) or connect it via the **USB-C to USB-A adapter**.

2. **Setting Up Display Preferences**:
   - ○ **Resolution & Screen Scaling**:
     You can adjust the **screen resolution** and **display scaling** in DeX mode for the best viewing experience. Go to **Settings > Display > Screen Resolution** to choose between **HD** or **WQHD** for better clarity. You can also adjust **screen scaling** to make text and icons larger or smaller depending on your preference.

   - ○ **Display Orientation**:
     DeX supports both **landscape** and **portrait** orientations. You can rotate the screen by simply adjusting the angle of your monitor or using the on-screen options in DeX mode. If you prefer to work in

portrait mode, go to **Settings** > **Display** and toggle the rotation settings to suit your needs.

○ **Taskbar Settings**:

You can further customize the **taskbar** in DeX by adding shortcuts to your most-used apps or adjusting its position. To access this, go to **Settings > Display > Taskbar**.

3. **Using Multiple Displays with DeX**:

○ If you're using **multiple displays** (e.g., a monitor and a secondary screen like a tablet or phone), you can extend the display or mirror the content across both screens. This feature enhances productivity by giving you more screen real estate to manage multiple tasks simultaneously.

4. **External Keyboard & Mouse Configuration**:

○ After connecting a **keyboard** and **mouse** via USB or Bluetooth, you can adjust settings for better control. Go to **Settings > Advanced Features > Input Devices** to configure hotkeys, mouse behavior, and keyboard shortcuts to improve your workflow.

Chapter 5

Camera

Camera Layout & Features

The **Samsung Galaxy Z Flip 6** is equipped with an advanced camera system designed to help you capture stunning photos and videos. Here's a look at the layout of the camera and its key features:

1. **Rear Camera Setup**:
   - **Main Camera**: The primary 12 MP wide camera offers fantastic photo quality with vibrant colors and detailed shots.

   - **Ultra-Wide Camera**: The 12 MP ultra-wide lens allows you to capture expansive landscapes, large group photos, and stunning architectural shots. The ultra-wide camera offers a 123-degree field of view.

   - **Flash**: The camera system features an LED flash to help you take better photos in low-light conditions.

2. **Front Camera (Selfie Camera)**:
   - The **10 MP front-facing camera** ensures that your selfies are sharp and clear, with features like **Live Focus** and **Wide Selfie Mode** to enhance your self-portrait shots.

3. **Camera Buttons & Controls**:
   - The camera app is user-friendly, featuring a large **capture button** at the bottom center for taking photos and videos.

   - On the screen, you'll find controls to toggle between the **wide** and **ultra-wide** cameras, access your gallery, and adjust settings like flash, timer, and aspect ratio.

4. **Camera Modes & Settings**:
   - The camera app offers various modes that can be accessed via the icons on the screen. You can switch between modes such as **Photo**, **Video**, **Pro**, **Live Focus**, and **Night Mode**.

Main Camera Functions & Flex Mode

The **main camera** on the Galaxy Z Flip 6 is packed with powerful features, and **Flex Mode** adds an extra layer of functionality to how you use the camera. Here's a breakdown:

1. **Using the Main Camera**:
   - The **12 MP wide camera** is perfect for everyday photography, delivering rich colors and sharp details. Whether you're taking portraits or landscape shots, the wide camera provides excellent clarity.

○ Tap the **shutter button** to take a photo. You can also hold it down for **burst mode**, which captures a series of images in quick succession.

2. **Flex Mode for Hands-Free Photography**:

   ○ **Flex Mode** allows you to take hands-free photos, which is especially useful for group selfies or creative angles. Simply fold your Galaxy Z Flip 6 to a 90-degree angle, and the screen will split into two.

   ○ In **Flex Mode**, the top half of the screen shows your camera viewfinder, and the bottom half is used for camera controls, such as zoom, timer, or shutter buttons.

   ○ **Hands-Free Features**: Place your Z Flip 6 on a flat surface, and it will remain in position, allowing you to take pictures or record videos without holding the device.

3. **Using Flex Mode for Group Shots**:

   ○ Flex Mode is ideal for taking group selfies or even video calls, as it lets you adjust the angle of the camera and keep the phone steady, offering a much wider field of view.

Taking Photos & Videos

The **Galaxy Z Flip 6's** camera system makes it easy to take professional-quality photos and videos. Here's how to maximize your photo and video capabilities:

1. **Taking Photos**:

○ **Single Shot**: In **Photo** mode, press the capture button to take a single shot. Your phone will automatically adjust for the best exposure, focus, and color balance.

○ **Burst Mode**: Hold down the capture button to take a series of photos rapidly. This is useful for capturing action shots or moments that require multiple frames.

○ **Zooming In and Out**: The Z Flip 6 offers both **digital zoom** and **ultra-wide zoom**. Pinch the screen to zoom in or out, or use the zoom slider to control the level of magnification.

2. **Taking Videos**:
   ○ Switch to **Video Mode** by tapping the camera mode icon at the bottom of the screen. Press the record button to start filming.

   ○ **Video Resolution**: The Z Flip 6 supports **4K video recording** at 30 or 60 frames per second (fps), allowing you to capture high-quality videos. You can change the resolution in the camera settings for the best video quality.

3. **Using Flex Mode for Video**:
   ○ Flex Mode is also perfect for recording videos hands-free. Position the phone on a surface, and the lower half of the screen will provide you with controls like **play/pause** and **stop recording**, while the top half displays your video feed.

Camera Modes: Portrait, Night, Pro Mode

Your **Samsung Galaxy Z Flip 6** comes with a variety of camera modes to help you achieve different types of shots. Here's a look at each mode:

1. **Portrait Mode**:
   - Portrait Mode creates a **blurred background effect**, also known as **bokeh**, to emphasize the subject of your photo, making it ideal for **portrait photography**. This mode works best with a person or an object close to the camera, with the background softly blurred.

   - You can adjust the **level of blur** and **lighting effects** in the settings. Portrait Mode also works with both the rear and front-facing cameras.

2. **Night Mode**:
   - **Night Mode** is designed for low-light conditions, where it enhances brightness and clarity in dimly lit environments. When activated, the phone takes multiple long-exposure shots and combines them to produce a clearer, brighter image with reduced noise.

   - Night Mode works best when the camera is stable and held steady during the shot. The Z Flip 6's **Optical Image Stabilization (OIS)** helps to reduce blur caused by hand movement during long exposures.

3. **Pro Mode**:

- **Pro Mode** gives you full control over the camera settings for more advanced users. This mode allows you to adjust **ISO**, **shutter speed**, **focus**, and **white balance** to achieve the perfect shot based on your environment and creative needs.

- Use **Pro Mode** for more control over your photos, especially in challenging lighting conditions. You can also save photos in **RAW format** for post-editing.

Editing & Sharing Photos

The **Samsung Galaxy Z Flip 6** not only lets you capture stunning photos and videos but also provides powerful tools for **editing** and **sharing** your media. Whether you want to make quick adjustments or add creative touches, the built-in editing tools and seamless sharing options make it easy to perfect and distribute your photos.

Basic Editing

After you've taken a photo or video, you can quickly edit it using the **Gallery** app, which comes pre-installed on your Galaxy Z Flip 6. Here are the basic editing tools you can use:

1. **Cropping and Rotating**:
   - Open the **Gallery** app and select the photo you want to edit.

   - Tap the **Edit** icon (the pencil) at the bottom of the screen.

○ To crop the photo, tap the **Crop** icon, adjust the corners to select the desired portion of the image, and tap **Done** to save the change.

○ To rotate the photo, tap the **Rotate** icon and rotate the image to your preferred orientation.

2. **Adjusting Brightness, Contrast, & Exposure**:

○ In the editing menu, you can adjust the **brightness**, **contrast**, and **exposure** to fine-tune the image. Swipe through the editing sliders to increase or decrease the intensity of each setting.

○ You can also adjust the **shadows** and **highlights** to balance light in the photo.

3. **Applying Filters**:

○ The **Filters** option allows you to apply various preset filters to your photos. Tap the **Filters** icon to scroll through a selection of looks, such as **Vivid**, **Warm**, or **Black & White**, and choose the one that best fits the vibe you're going for.

○ You can adjust the intensity of the filter for more or less effect.

4. **Adding Text or Drawings**:

○ You can add **text** to your photo by tapping the **Text** icon and typing your message. Choose from a variety of fonts, sizes, and colors to personalize your image.

○ To draw on the photo, tap the **Draw** icon. Select a brush size and color, then freely draw on the photo to add fun touches or annotations.

5. **Auto Enhance**:

○ For quick edits, you can use the **Auto Enhance** feature. This option automatically adjusts the image's brightness, contrast, and saturation to make it look its best with just one tap.

Social Media Integration

Once your photos are edited, sharing them on **social media** platforms is quick and easy with the **Gallery app**. Here's how to share your media seamlessly across your favorite social networks:

1. **Sharing to Social Media**:

○ After editing your photo, tap the **Share** icon (represented by three connected dots or a square with an upward arrow) in the editing menu.

○ You'll see a list of options for sharing, including popular apps like **Facebook**, **Instagram**, **Twitter**, **WhatsApp**, **Snapchat**, and more. Tap on the app you want to share the photo to.

○ You can then write a caption, tag friends, and add hashtags (depending on the platform) before posting the photo.

2. **Quick Sharing via Link**:

○ If you want to share a photo as a **link**, you can use **Google Photos** or **Samsung Cloud** to create a shareable link. Tap the **Share** icon, then select **Create Link**.

○ Copy the link and share it via text, email, or any messaging app.

3. **Direct Sharing to Multiple Platforms**:

○ You can share your photo to multiple social media platforms at once by selecting the relevant apps in the sharing menu. Some platforms, such as **Facebook** and **Instagram**, allow you to share directly from the Gallery app without needing to open the app separately.

4. **Sharing Videos**:

○ Videos can be shared in the same way as photos. Open the **Gallery** app, select the video you wish to share, and tap the **Share** icon. Select the social media platform or messaging app you want to use and follow the same steps to post or send the video.

5. **Creating Stories**:

○ Many platforms, such as **Instagram** and **Facebook**, offer **Story** features, where you can post photos or videos that disappear after 24 hours. After editing your photo, tap the **Story** icon in the sharing menu, and it will automatically open in the selected app where you can further customize the story with stickers, text, and effects.

6. **Emailing Photos**:

o You can also email your photos directly from the Gallery. Tap the **Share** icon, select **Email**, and enter the recipient's email address. Attach any additional files or messages before sending.

Chapter 6

Advanced Features & Customization

Fingerprint & Face Recognition Setup

Your **Samsung Galaxy Z Flip 6** offers **biometric security features** to make unlocking your device quick and secure. With **Fingerprint Recognition** and **Face Recognition**, you can easily access your phone without needing to type in a password or PIN. Here's how to set them up:

1. **Setting Up Fingerprint Recognition**:
   - Go to **Settings > Biometrics and security > Fingerprints**

   - Tap **Add fingerprint** and follow the on-screen instructions. You will be asked to place your finger on the **power button** (which doubles as the fingerprint scanner).

   - Keep lifting and placing your finger on the sensor until your fingerprint is fully registered.

   - Once your fingerprint is set up, you can use it to unlock your phone, authorize payments, and more.

2. **Setting Up Face Recognition**:

○ Go to **Settings > Biometrics and security > Face recognition**.

○ Tap **Register face** and follow the on-screen instructions to set up your face unlock. You'll need to position your face in front of the camera and make sure it's well-lit.

○ After registration, you can use Face Recognition to unlock your phone or access secure apps.

3. **Using Biometrics for App Security**:
   ○ Both **Fingerprint** and **Face Recognition** can be used to access specific apps or secure folders. Go to **Settings > Biometrics and security** and select **App lock** or **Secure Folder** to customize app protection with your biometrics.

4. **Managing Biometrics Settings**:
   ○ You can manage, delete, or add more fingerprints or faces at any time by returning to the **Biometrics and security** settings. You can also adjust the security level to prevent unauthorized access.

Security Features for Quick Unlock

Your Galaxy Z Flip 6 is designed to keep your data secure while providing a **fast and convenient unlocking experience**. Here's a rundown of key security features for quick unlocking:

1. **Quick Unlock with Fingerprint and Face Recognition**:

○ Once set up, your fingerprint and face are all you need to unlock your phone in seconds. Simply place your finger on the **power button** or look at the screen to unlock your phone instantly.

2. **Screen Lock Options**:
   ○ You can customize your screen lock to suit your preferences. Go to **Settings > Lock Screen** to choose from several lock options:

      ■ **Pattern Lock**: Draw a specific pattern to unlock your phone.

      ■ **PIN**: Enter a 4-6 digit number to unlock.

      ■ **Password**: Use a combination of numbers, letters, and symbols for added security.

   ○ **Smart Lock**:

      ■ Smart Lock allows you to unlock your phone in specific conditions, like when you're at home or when connected to a trusted Bluetooth device (such as your car). Enable **Smart Lock** in **Settings > Lock Screen > Smart Lock** to configure these options.

3. **Privacy and Security Settings**:
   ○ In **Settings > Biometrics and security**, you can manage permissions for sensitive apps, set up encryption, and control which apps can access your personal data.

Battery Management & Power Saving

Your **Samsung Galaxy Z Flip 6** comes with several features to help you manage battery life and maximize its efficiency. Here's how to make the most of your device's battery:

1. **Viewing Battery Usage**:
   - Go to **Settings > Device care > Battery** to see how much battery each app is consuming. You can also check the remaining battery percentage and time left until the next charge.

   - If an app is using excessive power, you can restrict its background activity or uninstall it if it's unnecessary.

2. **Battery Health**:
   - The **Battery Health** option in **Settings** provides information on your battery's performance and usage patterns over time. It helps you monitor your battery's health and suggests ways to extend its lifespan.

Optimizing Battery Usage & Using Power Saving Modes

1. **Optimizing Battery Usage**:
   - **Adaptive Battery**:
   Enable **Adaptive Battery** in **Settings > Battery**. This feature helps your phone learn your usage patterns and restricts battery usage for apps you don't use often, thereby conserving power.

- ○ **App Power Monitor**:

  In **Settings > Battery**, use the **App power monitor** to identify apps that consume excessive power and restrict or disable them when not in use.

- ○ **Background App Management**:

  Limit the number of apps running in the background to prevent them from draining your battery. Go to **Settings > Apps** to view and close apps running in the background.

2. **Power Saving Modes**: The **Galaxy Z Flip 6** offers several **power-saving modes** that can significantly extend your battery life:

   - ○ **Battery Saver**:

     This mode helps extend your phone's battery life by limiting background data, lowering screen brightness, and disabling certain features. To enable it, swipe down the **Quick Settings** panel and tap **Battery Saver**.

     - ■ **Customizing Battery Saver**:

       In **Settings > Battery**, tap **Power saving mode** to choose how you want to save power (e.g., reduce screen brightness, limit background apps).

   - ○ **Extreme Power Saving Mode**:

     If your battery is running critically low, **Extreme Power Saving Mode** reduces functionality even further to extend battery life. It limits your phone to basic apps like messaging, phone calls, and web browsing. To activate it, go to **Settings** > **Battery** > **Power saving mode**, and enable **Maximum power saving**.

3. **Fast Charging & Wireless Charging**:
   ○ **Fast Charging**:

   Your Z Flip 6 supports **fast charging** through the USB-C cable. To enable this feature, use the compatible **fast charger** included with your device.

   ○ **Wireless Charging**:

   For wireless charging, simply place your device on a **Qi-compatible wireless charger**. Fast wireless charging is supported for even quicker top-ups.

4. **Managing Battery Usage When Using DeX**:
   ○ When using **Samsung DeX** for a desktop experience, battery life can drain quickly due to the increased power usage. If you're using DeX for extended periods, keep your device plugged into a charger or consider enabling **Power Saving Mode** while using it.

App & Storage Management

Managing your apps and storage on the **Samsung Galaxy Z Flip 6** is essential for maintaining optimal performance and ensuring you have enough space for important files. Here's how to keep your device organized:

Monitoring Storage & Using External Storage

1. **Monitoring Storage**:

    ○ To check how much storage you're using and what's taking up space, go to **Settings > Battery and device care > Storage**. You'll see a breakdown of your used and available storage, with categories like **Apps**, **Images**, **Videos**, **Audio**, and **Documents**.

    ○ You can easily manage storage by tapping on each category to see which apps or files are consuming the most space.

    ○ **Clear Cache**: Under **Settings > Battery and device care > Storage**, you'll also find an option to **Clear Cache**, which helps free up space by removing unnecessary cached files from apps.

2. **Using External Storage**:

    ○ If you find that you're running low on internal storage, the Galaxy Z Flip 6 supports **microSD cards** (if applicable) to extend your available storage.

        ■ To insert a **microSD card**, locate the SIM tray, and insert the card into the designated slot.

        ■ Once the card is inserted, go to **Settings > Battery and device care > Storage** to see the external storage listed along with your device's internal storage.

    ○ **Managing Files on External Storage**:
        You can move files like photos, videos, or documents to external

storage by selecting them in **Samsung's My Files** app and choosing the **Move** or **Copy** option.

3. **Managing Apps**:

   ○ If you need more space, consider uninstalling apps that you rarely use. Go to **Settings > Apps**, tap on an app, and select **Uninstall**. You can also disable certain pre-installed apps that you don't use frequently.

   ○ **App Cache and Data**:

   In **Settings > Apps**, tap an app and choose **Storage**. Here, you can clear the app's cache (which may help free up space) or delete its data to reset the app to its default settings.

Notifications & Sounds

The **Samsung Galaxy Z Flip 6** allows you to customize your **notifications** and **sounds** to make sure you never miss an important alert while tailoring your experience. Here's how to manage and personalize your notification settings:

Customizing Alerts & Ringtones

1. **Customizing Notification Sounds**:

   ○ Go to **Settings > Sounds and vibration > Notification sound** to choose a custom notification sound for incoming alerts, such as messages, emails, or app notifications.

○ You can select from the default notification tones or pick a custom sound from your files. Tap **Add sound** to browse your stored files and choose a specific audio file for notifications.

2. **Setting Ringtone for Calls**:

   ○ To customize your ringtone for incoming calls, go to **Settings > Sounds and vibration > Ringtone**.

   ○ You can choose from the preset ringtones or select a custom ringtone from your **Sound Picker**. You can even set a specific ringtone for individual contacts by tapping on the contact in **Contacts > Edit** and then selecting **Ringtone**.

3. **Vibration Settings**:

   ○ You can adjust how your phone vibrates when receiving notifications or calls. Go to **Settings > Sounds and vibration > Vibration intensity**, where you can set the vibration strength for different alerts (e.g., calls, messages, etc.).

   ○ If you prefer a more subtle notification, you can also toggle the **Vibrate on Ring** or **Vibrate on Silent** options in **Settings > Sounds and vibration**.

4. **Do Not Disturb Mode**:

   ○ **Do Not Disturb** mode helps you mute notifications for a set period. To enable it, swipe down from the top of the screen and tap the **Do Not Disturb** icon. You can also go to **Settings > Notifications > Do**

not disturb to schedule the mode or allow exceptions for specific contacts or apps.

- ○ You can schedule **Do Not Disturb** mode to automatically activate at certain times, such as during bedtime or meetings, to ensure you're not disturbed.

5. **App-Specific Notification Settings**:
   - ○ Customize the notifications you receive from specific apps. Go to **Settings > Apps**, select an app, and tap **Notifications**. From here, you can enable or disable notifications for that app, adjust its sound, and determine whether it shows on the lock screen, banner notifications, or within the notification drawer.

6. **Pop-up Notifications**:
   - ○ If you prefer to see notifications in a pop-up window instead of a banner, go to **Settings > Notifications > Pop-up notifications**, and select the apps where you want to receive pop-up alerts. This setting is great for multitasking, as it allows notifications to appear without interrupting what you're doing.

7. **Advanced Sound & Vibration Options**:
   - ○ In **Settings > Sounds and vibration**, you can adjust **sound quality** and **effects**, which are powered by **Dolby Atmos** for an immersive audio experience. You can switch between different modes, including **Standard**, **Movie**, and **Music**, to adjust sound output depending on

what you're listening to.

- Additionally, you can fine-tune the **equalizer** for more control over the audio output, providing the best sound experience based on your preference.

Chapter 7

Troubleshooting

Resolving Common Issues

While your **Samsung Galaxy Z Flip 6** is designed for optimal performance, there may be times when you encounter minor issues. Here are some common problems and their solutions:

1. **Slow Performance**:
   - **Close Background Apps**: If your device is running slowly, check for apps running in the background that may be consuming resources. Swipe up from the bottom to view open apps and swipe away the apps you no longer need.

   - **Clear Cache**: Go to **Settings > Apps**, select an app, then tap **Storage** and choose **Clear Cache** to remove temporary files that might be slowing down your phone.

   - **Free Up Storage**: Check your device storage by going to **Settings > Battery and device care > Storage**. Delete or move unnecessary files and apps to free up space.

2. **Battery Draining Quickly**:

o **Optimize Battery Usage**: Go to **Settings > Battery and device care > Battery**, and tap **Optimize** to turn on battery-saving features.

o **Disable Power-Hungry Apps**: In **Battery > Battery Usage**, check which apps are consuming the most power. Consider disabling or limiting their background activity.

3. **App Crashes**:

   o **Update Apps**: Ensure your apps are up to date by going to the **Google Play Store** or **Galaxy Store**, then tap **My apps & games** to check for pending updates.

   o **Clear App Data**: If an app keeps crashing, go to **Settings > Apps**, select the app, and tap **Storage**. Choose **Clear Data** to reset the app.

4. **Connectivity Issues**:

   o **Wi-Fi Connection Problems**: If your device is having trouble connecting to Wi-Fi, try forgetting the network and reconnecting. Go to **Settings > Connections > Wi-Fi**, tap the network, and select **Forget**. Then reconnect by entering the Wi-Fi password.

   o **Bluetooth Issues**: Ensure that Bluetooth is turned on by going to **Settings > Connections > Bluetooth**. If a device isn't connecting, unpair and repair it.

   o **Mobile Data Problems**: If you're unable to use mobile data, make sure it's enabled in **Settings > Connections > Data usage**. You can also check with your carrier to ensure there are no service outages or restrictions.

Screen, Audio & Connectivity Problems

At times, you may encounter problems with your **screen**, **audio**, or **connectivity**. Here's how to resolve them:

1. **Screen Issues**:
   - **Unresponsive Touchscreen**: If your screen is not responding to touch, ensure the **screen protector** is not affecting sensitivity. You can restart your phone, or if the issue persists, try a soft reset (explained below).

   - **Flickering or Dim Display**: If your screen flickers or appears too dim, check your **brightness settings** in **Settings > Display** and turn on **Adaptive Brightness**. If the issue persists, try a soft reset or check for any software updates that may resolve the issue.

2. **Audio Issues**:
   - **No Sound or Low Volume**: Ensure that your **volume** is turned up and that the phone is not on **Silent** or **Do Not Disturb** mode. You can adjust volume settings from the **Quick Settings** panel or **Settings > Sounds and vibration**.

   - **Speaker Problems**: If you're having trouble with the speaker, ensure there's no debris blocking the speaker grill. You can clean the speaker gently with a soft cloth. If the problem persists, try restarting your phone.

○ **Bluetooth Audio Problems**: If you're unable to hear audio through your Bluetooth device, make sure it's properly paired and connected. Go to **Settings > Connections > Bluetooth**, and reconnect your Bluetooth device.

3. **Connectivity Issues**:

○ **Wi-Fi Problems**: If you're experiencing connection issues with Wi-Fi, try switching between **2.4GHz** and **5GHz** bands for better performance. You can also toggle **Airplane mode** on and off to reset the connection.

○ **Mobile Network Problems**: If you're having trouble connecting to your mobile network, check if **Airplane mode** is on. You can also try toggling **Data Roaming** on and off in **Settings > Connections > Mobile Networks**.

○ **Bluetooth Pairing Issues**: Ensure both devices are discoverable and in pairing mode. If needed, unpair and repair the devices through **Settings > Connections > Bluetooth**.

Resetting Your Device

If troubleshooting doesn't resolve the issues you're facing, a **reset** may be necessary. The **Samsung Galaxy Z Flip 6** offers several types of resets, including a **soft reset**, **hard reset**, and **factory reset**. Each of these can help resolve performance issues, but they vary in terms of the data they affect.

Soft & Hard Resets, Factory Reset

1. **Soft Reset**: A **soft reset** is essentially restarting your device. It's helpful when your phone is sluggish, or apps are behaving erratically. A soft reset does not erase any data.

   ○ To perform a **soft reset**, press and hold the **Power button** and the **Volume Down button** at the same time until the **Samsung logo** appears on the screen. Release both buttons, and the device will restart.

2. **Hard Reset**: A **hard reset** is used when your device is unresponsive and doesn't react to a normal soft reset. This can help when the device is frozen or stuck.

   ○ To perform a **hard reset**, press and hold the **Power button** and **Volume Down button** for about **10 seconds** until the device vibrates and restarts.

   ○ A hard reset will force the phone to reboot, but it will not erase your data.

3. **Factory Reset**: A **factory reset** restores your phone to its original settings, erasing all your data, apps, and customizations. This is a useful step when you're troubleshooting persistent issues or preparing the device for sale or transfer. Before performing a factory reset, make sure to back up your data.

   ○ To perform a **factory reset**, go to **Settings > General management > Reset > Factory data reset**.

   ○ Follow the on-screen instructions to complete the process. This will erase all your personal data, settings, and apps, returning the phone to its factory settings.

   ○ If you can't access the settings, you can also reset the device from recovery mode by turning the device off and pressing and holding the **Volume Up button** + **Power button** simultaneously until the Samsung logo appears. In recovery mode, select **Wipe data/factory reset** using the volume buttons, then confirm with the power button.

Getting Help

If you encounter issues that can't be resolved through troubleshooting or resets, or if you simply need more assistance, **Samsung Support** is available to provide help. Here's how you can get the support you need:

Contacting Samsung Support

Samsung offers several ways to get in touch with their support team for personalized help. Whether it's a technical question or a product issue, you can reach out through these methods:

1. **Samsung Support Website**:
   ○ You can access a wealth of self-help resources, FAQs, manuals, and troubleshooting guides for your Galaxy Z Flip 6 directly through the Samsung support website. Search for specific issues or check the **Product FAQs** to find immediate solutions to common questions.

2. **Phone Support**:
   ○ To speak directly with a **Samsung customer service representative**, you can call the customer service hotline. In most regions, the contact number can be found in the **Contact Us** section of the Samsung website or within the **Samsung Members** app on your device.

   ○ The customer support team can assist you with product inquiries, technical assistance, warranty questions, and more.

3. **Live Chat**:
   ○ **Samsung Live Chat** offers real-time assistance directly on the Samsung website. You can chat with an agent for quick answers to your questions without needing to pick up the phone.

   ○ Simply visit the **Support section** on the Samsung website and select the **Live Chat** option.

4. **Samsung Members App**:

   ○ The **Samsung Members** app is an invaluable tool for troubleshooting, getting support, and interacting with Samsung's support team.

   ○ Open the **Samsung Members app** on your Galaxy Z Flip 6 and tap the **Support** tab to access troubleshooting tools, FAQs, and even initiate a live chat with a representative.

   ○ The app also provides easy access to product guides, updates, and tips tailored to your specific device.

Accessing Community Forums

Sometimes, other **Samsung Galaxy Z Flip 6** users may have already experienced and solved similar issues, and the **Samsung Community Forums** is a great place to find peer-driven solutions and tips. Here's how you can access and use the forums:

1. **Samsung Community**:

   ○ Visit **Samsung's online Community Forums** to find answers from other users. You can search for discussions related to your problem or ask a question of your own.

   ○ The community is filled with users who share tips, troubleshooting advice, and creative solutions based on their own experiences with the device. It's an excellent resource when you're looking for solutions or want to learn more about your Galaxy Z Flip 6.

Bonus

Frequently Asked Questions

What's the Difference Between the Main & Cover Display?

The **Main Display** is the large 6.7-inch **Dynamic AMOLED 2X** screen that unfolds to provide a full-screen experience. It's perfect for watching videos, gaming, browsing the web, and multitasking with apps. On the other hand, the **Cover Display** is the smaller external screen located on the front of the phone when it's folded. It allows you to quickly check notifications, time, and basic information, and even interact with certain apps like music or messages without opening the device. The Cover Display is mainly for quick tasks, while the Main Display is ideal for full-screen use.

How Do I Extend Battery Life on My Z Flip 6?

To extend battery life on your Galaxy Z Flip 6, you can:

1. **Enable Power Saving Mode**: Go to **Settings > Battery** and turn on **Power Saving Mode** to limit background processes and reduce battery consumption.

2. **Use Adaptive Battery**: Turn on **Adaptive Battery** in **Settings > Battery** to limit power-hungry apps that you don't use frequently.

3. **Adjust Screen Brightness**: Lower the screen brightness or enable **Adaptive Brightness** to adjust brightness based on ambient light.

4. **Disable Unused Features**: Turn off features like **Bluetooth**, **Wi-Fi**, or **Location Services** when not in use.

5. **Limit Background Apps**: Use **Developer Options** to limit background processes and save power.

6. **Manage App Power**: Go to **Settings > Battery** to monitor which apps use the most power and adjust settings accordingly.

Can I Use My Z Flip 6 in the Rain?

The **Samsung Galaxy Z Flip 6** has an **IPX8 rating**, which means it's resistant to water immersion up to 1.5 meters for up to 30 minutes. While this makes it resistant to water exposure, it's not fully protected against **rain** or **splashing**. If you're caught in the rain, it's okay, but you should avoid prolonged exposure to water, especially submersion, as this may damage the device over time. Always wipe off any moisture and avoid using the phone if it gets wet.

How Do I Set Up Dual SIM?

To set up **Dual SIM** on your Galaxy Z Flip 6:

1. Insert two SIM cards into the **SIM tray** (if your model supports dual SIM).

2. Go to **Settings > Connections > SIM card manager**.

3. You can now select which SIM you want to use for calls, messages, and mobile data.

4. Customize the settings for each SIM, including choosing a default SIM for data usage or setting up your SIM preferences.

5. You can switch between SIM cards as needed for calls or data by adjusting the **SIM settings** in **Settings > Connections**.

Can I Connect My Z Flip 6 to a TV or Monitor?

Yes, you can connect your **Galaxy Z Flip 6** to a TV or monitor using **Samsung DeX** or **HDMI adapters**:

1. **Using Samsung DeX**:

   Samsung DeX allows you to use your phone as a desktop experience. To connect wirelessly, ensure both devices are on the same Wi-Fi network and use **DeX** from the quick settings or **Settings > Connections > DeX**. You can also connect your device to a monitor via a **USB-C to HDMI cable** or **DeX Pad** for a wired connection.

2. **Using an HDMI Adapter**:

   You can connect your Galaxy Z Flip 6 to a monitor or TV using a **USB-C to HDMI adapter**. Plug the adapter into your phone and connect it to the HDMI port of your TV or monitor. Once connected, you can mirror your phone's screen or use it for media playback, gaming, and more.

Appendices

Warranty & Legal Information

Understanding your **warranty coverage** and **legal rights** is important when you purchase a Samsung Galaxy Z Flip 6. Here's what you need to know:

1. **Warranty Coverage & Terms**:
   - Your Samsung Galaxy Z Flip 6 comes with a **limited warranty** that covers defects in materials and workmanship for a specified period (typically one year) from the date of purchase. This warranty covers repairs and replacement of defective parts under normal use.

   - The warranty does not cover damage caused by accidents, unauthorized repairs, misuse, or environmental factors like water damage (unless your device has a specific **IP rating** for water resistance).

   - To ensure you're covered, always keep your **proof of purchase** and check Samsung's official warranty policy for details on eligibility and the process for making a claim.

2. **What's Covered Under Warranty**:
   - **Manufacturing Defects**: Issues with the phone due to faulty manufacturing, such as non-functioning buttons, display problems, or internal malfunctions.

o **Hardware Failures**: If the phone's hardware components, such as the camera, battery, or charging port, fail due to factory defects.

3. **What's Not Covered**:

   o **Accidental Damage**: Damage from drops, impacts, water exposure (unless covered by an IP rating), or any damage caused by external forces.

   o **Software Issues**: Problems caused by third-party apps or software issues that are not Samsung-related.

   o **Battery Wear**: Battery wear over time, which is considered a normal part of device usage.

Regulatory & Safety Information

Your **Samsung Galaxy Z Flip 6** meets various **regulatory standards** and complies with safety guidelines to ensure that it is safe to use.

1. **Regulatory Compliance**:

   o The Galaxy Z Flip 6 complies with various local and international standards, including:

      ▪ **FCC (Federal Communications Commission)** in the United States

- **CE Marking** for European Union compliance

- **SAR (Specific Absorption Rate)** for electromagnetic radiation safety

o It is also compliant with safety regulations for wireless devices, ensuring it doesn't interfere with other electronics or emit harmful radiation.

2. **Safety Information**:

o Always use **Samsung-approved chargers** and accessories to avoid damage or safety hazards.

o Avoid exposing your device to extreme temperatures (e.g., direct sunlight or freezing conditions) to prevent battery issues or device malfunction.

o Never attempt to open or modify your phone's internal components, as this could void your warranty and cause injury or damage.

o Keep your phone out of reach of small children to avoid choking hazards from small parts, such as the SIM card tray or the charging port.

3. **Environmental Considerations**:

- Samsung encourages recycling and reducing the environmental impact of electronic waste. You can recycle your old Samsung devices through certified recycling programs.

Glossary

Here are some key terms and definitions to help you better understand your **Samsung Galaxy Z Flip 6**:

1. **AMOLED (Active Matrix Organic Light Emitting Diode):**
   - A display technology that offers vibrant colors, deep blacks, and efficient energy use. The Galaxy Z Flip 6 features a **Dynamic AMOLED 2X** display, providing sharp images and fast refresh rates.

2. **Flex Mode:**
   - A feature unique to foldable devices like the Z Flip 6, allowing the phone to bend at a 90-degree angle and use the upper and lower halves of the screen independently for multitasking and hands-free operation.

3. **IP Rating:**
   - The **Ingress Protection (IP) rating** is a standard that defines how well a device is protected from dust and water. The Z Flip 6 has an **IPX8** rating, meaning it is resistant to water immersion (up to 1.5 meters for 30 minutes) but not fully protected against dust.

4. **DeX (Desktop Experience):**

- Samsung DeX allows your Galaxy device to be used as a desktop computer by connecting it to a monitor, keyboard, and mouse. This feature provides a PC-like experience for productivity tasks.

5. **SAR (Specific Absorption Rate)**:
   - The **SAR** measures the amount of radiofrequency energy absorbed by the body when using the device. The Z Flip 6 complies with **SAR limits** set by regulatory authorities to ensure user safety.

6. **NFC (Near Field Communication)**:
   - **NFC** is a technology that enables devices to communicate with each other over short distances, typically used for contactless payments or transferring data between devices.

7. **SIM (Subscriber Identity Module)**:
   - A small card that stores information related to your mobile network, such as your phone number, contacts, and carrier settings. The Z Flip 6 supports **Dual SIM**, allowing you to use two different phone numbers at the same time.

8. **5G**:
   - The latest generation of **mobile network technology**, offering faster download and upload speeds, lower latency, and improved connection reliability compared to 4G LTE.

9. **Wireless PowerShare**:

○ A feature that allows you to share your phone's battery power with other devices, like wireless earbuds or another phone, by using reverse wireless charging.